Howell-Ap-Howell

The Birthplace and Childhood of Napoleon

Howell-Ap-Howell

The Birthplace and Childhood of Napoleon

ISBN/EAN: 9783337350567

Printed in Europe, USA, Canada, Australia, Japan

Cover: Foto ©ninafisch / pixelio.de

More available books at **www.hansebooks.com**

The Birthplace and Childhood of Napoleon.

BY
HOWELL-AP-HOWELL.

Illustrated by 18 photographs taken on the spot by G. E. THOMPSON, *author of* "Around the Roman Campagna" *etc.*

"Youth, what man's age is like to be, doth show;
We may our ends by our beginnings know"
Denham.

EDWARD HOWELL,
CHURCH STREET,
LIVERPOOL.
MDCCCXCVI.

CONTENTS.

CHAPTER I.
THE ISLAND OF CORSICA — — —   1

CHAPTER II.
THE FRENCH IN CORSICA — — — — — —   5

CHAPTER III.
HISTORY OF CORSICA — — — — — —   13

CHAPTER IV.
PAOLI — — — — —   22

CHAPTER V.
AJACCIO — — — — — — —   30

CHAPTER VI.
THE HOUSE OF THE BUONAPARTES — — — —   36

CHAPTER VII.
NAPOLEON — — —   40

CHAPTER VIII.
NAPOLEON'S CHILDHOOD — — —   44

CHAPTER IX.
NAPOLEON'S SCHOOLDAYS — —   49

LIST OF ILLUSTRATIONS

	PAGE.
AJACCIO	*Frontispiece*
GRAND HOTEL IN AJACCIO	12
TOMB OF KING THEODORE IN SOHO, LONDON	21
BUST OF NAPOLEON BY CANOVA	29
AVENUE LEADING FROM THE QUAY OF AJACCIO	30
COURS NAPOLEON, AJACCIO	31
STATUE OF NAPOLEON	32
NAPOLEON—*(Bronze cast after death)*	34
HOUSE OF THE BUONAPARTES	35
MADAME LETITIA'S SPINET IN HOUSE OF THE BUONAPARTES	37
THE OFFICE OF HIS FATHER *(Charles Buonaparte)* IN DITTO	37
SEDAN CHAIR BELONGING TO MADAME LETITIA IN DITTO	37
ROOM WHERE NAPOLEON WAS BORN IN DITTO	37
TERRACE ON THE ROOF OF DITTO	38
BALL ROOM IN DITTO	38
BUST OF MADAME LETITIA *(Napoleon's Mother)*	41
NAPOLEON'S GROTTO, AJACCIO	52
PLAQUE OF NAPOLEON *(when a young man)* by DAVID OF ANGERS	53

PREFACE.

LANFREY, *in his* "Vie de Napoléon" *says* "*that the childhood and youth of great men necessarily elude history, for the reason that youth, with its secret transformations and psychological mysteries, is a difficult study, and one in which very few certain ideas can be formed even by the most attentive observer. It is an age of growth, in which the whole man is changing and unsettled.*" *This is true, yet the childhood of Napoleon was marked by many traits of character which, in mature development, can be traced back to early infancy, and however trivial some of the incidents may seem, still the trite saying of Wordsworth, that "the child is father to the man," is amply exemplified.*

In the following pages I have endeavoured to throw more light on his early years, by gathering together from various sources all that appears to be known respecting him. The description of the house of the "Buonapartes" in Ajaccio is taken from notes made by Mr. G. E. Thompson during a tour through Corsica in 1894. The illustrations from photographs by his camera, of the interior of the house and Napoleonic relics, form the chief interest of the work, for " writing a book is like building a house. A man forms a plan, and collects materials; he thinks he has enough to raise a large and stately edifice; but after he has arranged, compacted and polished, his work turns out to be but a very small performance."

HOWELL-AP-HOWELL.

28 CHURCH STREET,
        LIVERPOOL.

THE BIRTHPLACE AND CHILDHOOD OF NAPOLEON.

CHAPTER I.

THE ISLAND OF CORSICA.

THE Island of Corsica is about twenty leagues from the coast of Tuscany, forty from that of Provençe, and sixty from that of Spain. Its surface is fifteen hundred square miles in extent, and it contains four maritime towns, Bastia, Calvi, Ajaccio, and Bonifaccio.

A chain of lofty mountains runs through the centre of the island, and some of its highest peaks are perpetually snow-clad. On the east coast, from Bastia to Aleria, there is a stretch of level country about sixty miles in length, and from ten to twelve in breadth, extensively covered with forests; the mountains are clothed with chesnut trees, and the valleys filled with olive, mulberry, orange, lemon, and other fruit trees; on the tops of the hills are forests of pine, fir, and evergreen oaks. Oil, wine, and silk are the three staple commodities most suitable for exportation. In the winter months the climate is most enjoyable, but in the heat of the summer it is very dry, and the scarcity of water drives the inhabitants to the hills, whence they descend again in the winter, either to graze their flocks, or to cultivate the plains.

On the coast, cereals and Indian corn are grown in abundance. The mulberry tree is cultivated to great perfection in the valleys, and as the climate is suited both to its growth and to the rearing of silk-worms, there is a great opening for this important industry. The vine also is cultivated with great success, and admirable wine is made of rather a full bodied character. Higher up, the chesnut tree grows to a magnificent size, and produces fruit of the very best quality. Entire districts, especially on the eastern side of the island, are covered with splendid chesnut forests. During many centuries of tyranny and oppression, the Corsicans owed their subsistence principally to the chesnut tree, with assistance from the oil of the olive tree, the wine of their vines, and the flesh and milk of their sheep.

They might be hemmed in on all sides in their mountain fastnesses; all egress might be stopped for years, and yet they flourished. These times have passed away, and from the end of the last century there has been peace in Corsica; still many of the inhabitants retain their desultory habits. They live in sober idleness, play at cards, talk politics all day, and work as little as they possibly can. Their artificial modern wants, even, are supplied by the sale of their surplus crops, now rendered easy by the increased facility of communication with the continent.

The cultivation of the olive tree also appears to engender the same apathy and disinclination to work. From San Fiorenzo to Calvi, the lovely fertile valleys, in their luxuriance and richness of growth, enable the peasants to lead a *"far niente"* life of easy enjoyment.

The manufactures are in a poor state, and are confined to the most indispensable wants of trade and the common necessities of life; the women almost everywhere weave the coarse brown cloth, Panno Corso, also called Pelone; the herdsmen make cheese and the cheese-cake (Broccio); there are saltworks, but only in the Gulf of Porto-Vecchio. Sardines, tunnies, and coral are taken on many parts of the coast, but the fisheries are carried on in the same desultory fashion as the agriculture.

However melancholy be the general condition of Corsica, she is at least preserved by her thin population from the scourge of an abject and perishing class, which has produced in the great centres of civilisation of the continent far more terrible miseries than those of banditism and vengeance in Corsica.

CHAPTER II.

THE FRENCH IN CORSICA.

THE French have now been more than one hundred years in possession of Corsica, but they have never succeeded in closing and healing the great wound of the nation, nor have they, with all the resources of their civilisation, achieved more for the island than a few improvements. The island, which has twice given France her Emperor, and twice dictated laws to her, has gained nothing by it but the satisfaction of her revenge. The Corsican will never forget in what a shameful way France possessed herself of his country. When Gregorovius was travelling through the island he heard Corsicans railing bitterly at Genoa, and he said to them, "Let the old republic, Genoa, rest in peace, you have accomplished your vendetta upon her; Napoleon, a Corsican, has annihilated her. France deceived you, and deprived you of your nationality; you have had your vendetta upon France too, for you sent her a Corsican, Napoleon, who subjugated her, and even now that great country is a Corsican conquest, and your own province."

The Corsicans and the French are separated by a deep gulf of nationality, innermost nature, and sentiments. The Corsican is a decided Italian; his language avowedly one of the purest Italian dialects, and his nature, his soil, and his history, still link the wandering son to his former home. Indeed, the French feel themselves strangers in this island, and soldiers and officials regard their period of service there as a cheerless banishment to the "isle of goats." The Corsican cannot even understand a nature like the French, for he is serious, taciturn, chaste, consistent—a man in the best sense of the word, and firm as the granite of his mountains.

The entire heroic history of the Corsicans springs purely and singly from the natural law of the sacredness and inviolability of the family. All the virtues of the Corsicans spring from this spirit, and even the dread night-shades of their life, such as their family feuds and banditism, belong to this common root.

In many particulars the inhabitants differ largely from those of the countries which surround them on both sides of the Mediterranean. The very fact of their isolation, together with their stormy history, has tended to make them what they are at the present day.

The Corsicans complain very bitterly that they are neglected by France, and that the very great natural resources of the island are not developed as they might be. This reproach scarcely appears just. The first Napoleon, it is true, did but little for his native country. Perhaps he was so totally absorbed by his herculean duties that he had but little leisure to devote to the material welfare of so small a province; perhaps he was disinclined to draw, in too marked a manner, the attention of the France he governed to his Corsican origin. On one occasion a decree was signed for some important public works at Ajaccio, but they were not carried out. This he only learnt years afterwards. When at St. Helena, his thoughts, however, reverted constantly to the mountain island which gave him birth. He often spoke of it, and of what he intended to have accomplished for its welfare and prosperity had he remained in power.

Subsequent governments appear to have done for Corsica what they have done for other departments of France—perhaps even more. The French centralised system of law, education, and road making have been generally introduced, and every facility given to the inhabitants to mentally improve themselves, and thereby to lay down the foundation of public prosperity. The roads that now connect the principal coast towns, and encircle the island are excellent, in fact as good, even in the most wild and uninhabited regions, as the high roads in England. There is also a very good road intersecting the island from Bastia to Ajaccio. It passes over the two mountain chains, and through Corte, the ancient patriotic capital of Corsica. Various forest roads have lately been made, leading into the heart of the country, even into the primeval forests which occupy the high central regions.

The great impediment to the material progress of Corsica, up to a very recent period, has no doubt been the abnormal social condition of the island. The vendetta which characterises it must sap at the root of all public enterprise and prosperity. This system of blood vengeance has existed for hundreds of years, and was, until recently, recognised and approved by nearly the entire community, including even the less enlightened ministers of religion. Its origin is obscure, but may be traced to the feuds and warfares that existed in the island, dividing the members of families and of communities, ever arming one against the other, to the weakening of authority, and adding to the difficulty of obtaining justice.

All Corsicans carried fire-arms. If one man considered himself insulted by another in any way, however trivial the grounds, he shot him. From that moment the family of the man killed was bound in honour to pursue the murderer, or, in his default, some member of his family, and to retaliate blood for blood. This obligation descended from one member of the family to another, until it often ended in the almost entire destruction of both families. Villages, entire communities, would take up the quarrel of their members against other villages, other communities, and thus, in the absence of a public foe, they massacred each other.

It was in vain that the French government kept a regiment or two of soldiers in the island, and a large body of " moveable gendarmerie," accustomed to the mountains and to mountain warfare. The vendetta was too deeply rooted in the minds of the Corsicans. The mountains were too inaccessible, and the population too favourable to these " honourable bandits," for them to be exterminated from the land. In the year 1854, very extreme measures were adopted—measures which seem strange in our times as applied to a department of France, to the birthplace of the late imperial family.

Two laws were passed. By the one, the entire population was disarmed, and it was made penal to carry firearms, or arms of any description, for any reason whatever, even including the pursuit of game. A landed proprietor could not take out a gun to shoot a bird or a hare without the permission of the prefect. All the better informed inhabitants cheerfully acquiesced in the law for the benefit of the community. This law was partially repealed in 1869.

By the other law, *loi du recel*, or law of concealment, all persons harbouring or assisting outlaws became liable to imprisonment. This law was very effectually carried out in a most singular manner. If a man kills an enemy, and flies to the mountain, the authorities instantly seize and imprison his relatives and keep them in prison until he is caught, or has surrendered. Here is an instance; a bandit who had killed twenty-seven people in his life, principally gendarmes, and had been out in the mountains above thirty years, had been for some time lost sight of, and was supposed to have gone to Sardinia. He had recently reappeared, and had been seen in the vicinity of Sartene. As many as sixty of his relations and descendants were immediately seized and imprisoned, and were only released when it became quite evident that he had again withdrawn from the island.

However arbitrary this may seem, the result was most beneficial. These men of bronze, who killed an enemy as they would a noxious insect, whom no human or divine feeling could restrain from shedding blood, are fond fathers, sons, and brothers. They cannot bear to see their children, fathers and mothers, brothers and sisters in prison on their account, so, as a rule, give themselves up for punishment.

The rigid application of the *loi du recel* cuts at the root of one of the chief causes that tended to keep up banditism. The imprisonment of his relatives deprived the bandit of the all but indispensable assistance he was receiving, and transformed the members of his own family either into very lukewarm sympathizers, or absolute antagonists.

The women also sometimes avenged themselves, for as late as 1865, there were three women in prison for killing their lovers. In one case, a handsome girl of twenty shot her lover dead in the market place of Corte, because, after promising to marry her, he deserted her, and positively refused to ratify his engagement. Popular opinion was so strong in her favour that she suffered only three months' imprisonment!

The vigorous policy of these measures has at last told thoroughly on the social condition of the entire community, and security reigns where diffidence and alarm formerly existed; and as the island is now encircled with good roads, and regular and frequent steam communication between its principal ports and the French and Italian mainlands, the great natural resources ought speedily to be developed. Capital and enterprise alone are wanted.

In no part of Europe can a few weeks be more happily spent by the tourist than in Corsica, during the spring or autumn of the year. To some classes of invalids, Corsica offers winter resources, especially at Ajaccio, much more suitable than the Genoese Riviera.*

* In Ajaccio, some of the hotels have been recently erected—notably the "Grand," a noble building, facing the Cours Grandval—with magnificent gardens, luxuriantly covered with indigenous plants and trees; a thick wood covers the hill behind the house. Along the "Rue Grandval" there is the "Belle Vue," and in the great square the "Hotel de France." English is spoken at these hotels.

Grand Hotel in Ajaccio.

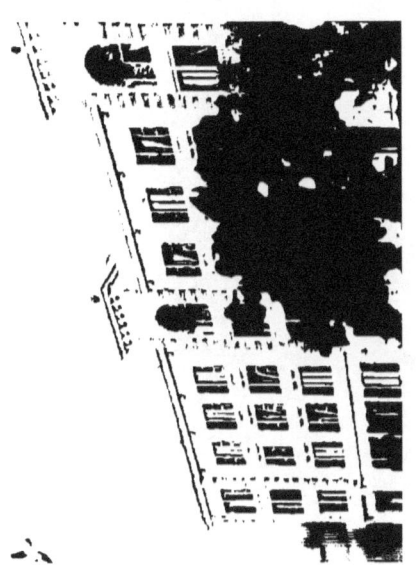

CHAPTER III.

History of Corsica.

A GLANCE over the history of Corsica will enable us to follow the various transitionary periods of an island which Rousseau declared was the only European land capable of movement, of law giving, and of peaceable renovation.

The first known inhabitants of Corsica were Phoceans from Asia Minor. They were followed by the Phœnicians and the Carthaginians. Then Rome sent her troops and built the towns of Mariana and Aleria. In 460 A.D., Corsica was conquered by the Vandals, and after they were driven out, and until 750, it was a dependency of the Greek Empire. About that time, the Saracens made Corsica their home, but in the ninth century, Charlemagne defeated them, and the island was granted to Boniface, Count of Tuscany. He it was, who founded the town of Bonifaccio. About the year 1000, many feudal lords arose and became powerful, but the people rebelled against them, and handed the country over to the pope. In 1081, Pope Urban II placed the island under the dominion of the Bishop of Pisa. This action roused the ire of the then powerful republic of Genoa—a people in a chronic state of enmity with their neighbours, the Pisans. The Genoese persuaded Pope Innocent II to let them have a half share in the Bishopric, but they very soon took the whole island. The Pisan government had been mild and just, but the history of Corsica during the four hundred years in which it was governed by the Genoese is replete with wars, bloodshed, tyrannical government and wrong doing.

The history of Corsica is full of heroes, of heroic deeds, of romantic achievements. Each successive century bore patriots ever ready to sacrifice their fortunes and their lives for their country, as in the heroic days of early Rome. Nor were the opportunities for doing so, wanting: no sooner was one enemy disposed of than another appeared.

Peace never lasted more than a few years, seldom as long; and each successive generation had thus to renew the struggles which had tested the courage, the patriotism, and the endurance of its precursor.

Is it surprising that the names of these Corsicans should be household words? that Giudice della Rocca, Giampolo, Sampiero, Paoli, and many others should live in the affections of the Corsicans to-day? Is it surprising that the women should have imbibed and shown, in times gone by, the stern patriotism of the women of Sparta? Their chants and national songs to the present day breathe a spirit of defiance and a love of vengeance unknown to the inhabitants of more peaceful regions.

A population which has for so many centuries—indeed until quite recently—lived in a state of constant warfare against foreign tyranny and oppression, cannot all at once calm down to the social condition of countries that have for centuries ceased to fight for their existence.

The Genoese were the most persistent and cruel persecutors of Corsica. War never ceased from their establishment on the island in the thirteenth century until the time that the Corsicans surrendered themselves to France in 1769, two months only before the birth of Napoleon Buonaparte. Can we wonder that a brave, strong, yet small nation of mountaineers, such as the Corsicans were and are, should after such a long period of government by many and diverse masters, after terrible persecutions and long wars, be proud, revengeful, and idle?

The islanders had again and again risen in revolt against their hard masters, for a succession of infamous governors—men who came from Genoa poor, and after two years' office returned rich—most cruelly oppressed them. By their ill-gotten wealth, and by their interest in the senate, they were able on their return to secure themselves against any inquiry into their conduct.

The Corsicans, like many other mountaineers, had always been too much given to private feuds. But it was charged against their Genoese masters that in their dread of union among their subjects, they themselves fomented dissensions. It was asserted that under the last sixteen governors no less than 26,000 Corsicans had died by the hands of the assassin.

In the legal proceedings that followed on these deeds of bloodshed, the Genoese judges found their profit. Condemnation was often followed by confiscation of the criminal's estates; acquittal had often been preceded by a heavy bribe to the judge. Multitudes were condemned to the galleys on frivolous charges in the hope that they would purchase their freedom at a high price. The law was even worse than the judges. A man could be condemned to the galleys or to death on secret information, without being once confronted with his accusers, without undergoing any examination, without the observance of any formality of any kind in the sentence passed on him. The judge could either acquit the greatest criminal, or condemn a man of stainless character. No wonder that Horace Walpole exclaimed "I hate the Genoese; they make a commonwealth the most devilish of all tyrannies!"

In 1729, the oppressive government of the Genoese caused an insurrection which ultimately led to their expulsion.

A lieutenant, whilst collecting taxes, refused the coin of a poor peasant, because it was a farthing light. The old man went off pondering and talking to himself; he complained to his friends, and they all talked indignantly of the state of the country. The angry feeling spread from place to place. It was resolved that no more taxes of any kind should be paid, and soon a war broke out, which lasted forty years. Another account is, that a taxgatherer demanded fivepence of a poor woman, and as she could not pay, abused her, and seized some of her furniture. She raised an outcry, her neighbours flocked in, and took her part. The taxgatherer used threats, and they replied with a volley of stones. Troops were sent to support him, and the people flew to their weapons. The insurrection spread, and soon the whole island was again in arms.

In the year 1736, a ship flying the British flag sailed into the port of Aleria, and in her there came a fine looking man, gorgeously attired in a long scarlet furred coat, attended by a retinue of two officers, a secretary, a chaplain, a steward, slaves and lackeys. The cargo of the ship consisted of 10 cannons, 7,000 muskets, 2,000 pairs of shoes, 7,000 sacks of corn, great quantities of ammunition, provisions of all kinds, as well as several chests full of gold and silver coins.

He was a German, named Theodore von Neuhoff, a baron of Westphalia; of all the adventurers of his remarkable day the most talented and most successful.

He had had experience of everything, seen everything, thought, endeavoured, enjoyed and suffered everything. Following his peculiar bent, he had run through all the possible forms in which happiness can appear to man, and had concluded with the idea that it must be desirable to a mind of power to be a king. By his indomitable efforts, he raised sums of money to provide this for poor struggling Corsica. He landed at a time when her need was greatest, and promised further help if the people would make him their ruler. The leading men of Corsica received him with great marks of honour, and as the poor people had, like the Jews of old in their despair, longed for a king who should deliver them from the Philistines, he was recognised and proclaimed king under the title of Theodore the First. Taking up his quarters in the Episcopal house at Cervione, he conducted everything in quite a royal style, so far as outward ceremonies were concerned, surrounded himself with guards and all princely ceremonial, and played the king as well as if born to the purple. Coins were struck in gold, silver and copper, on the obverse was a laurel-wreathed shield, over which was a crown with the letters T.D.G.; on the reverse, " Pro bono publico Corso." They were regarded with great curiosity on the continent, and are now very rare. Theodore worked hard in the interests of his kingdom, and for a time the people clung to him with unshaken fidelity, but at the end of about eight months, he perceived that they cooled in their affection towards him, for he had promised further help, which, however, never came, and he therefore wisely assembled the council and agreed to either resign his crown, or go to the continent at the end of the next month, if by that time, his promise was not fulfilled. In November he appointed a regency and left the Island to seek further aid.

Genoa, meanwhile, set a price upon his head. In the following year Theodore returned, bringing three ships, laden with supplies of every kind: landed under Dutch colours, and found his people somewhat estranged from him, and in treaty with the French. Again he left for the continent. In 1743, when nearly forgotten, he landed a third time with three English ships of war, well provided as before. He was coldly received, and heavy-hearted he sailed away for England never to return. When in London he was arrested for debt by some Genoese merchants, who put him in King's Bench prison.

He regained his liberty by registering his effects for the benefit of his creditors. He left them *solely* his already vanquished kingdom of Corsica. Quitting his prison in a sedan chair, he went to the Portuguese Embassy, but failing to find the Minister, and having no money, he asked the men to take him to a certain tailor in Soho. There he was taken in, and in a few days he died. John Wright, an oil

Tomb of King Theodore in Soho, London.

man, saved him from a pauper's funeral by burying him at his own expense. Horace Walpole wrote the epitaph on his tombstone in St. Anne's Churchyard,* Soho, which reads thus:

"Near this place is interred Theodore, King of Corsica, who died in this parish, December 11th, 1756, immediately after leaving King's Bench Prison, by the benefit of the Act of Insolvency, in consequence of which he registered his kingdom of Corsica for the use of his creditors.

  The Grave, great teacher, to a level brings
  Heroes and beggars, galley slaves and Kings.
  But Theodore this moral learn'd ere dead:
  Fate pour'd its lesson on his living head,
  Bestow'd a kingdom and denied him bread."

* It is most interesting to note that William Hazlitt, poet and essayist, who also wrote a *History of the Life of Napoleon*, lies buried near the same spot.

CHAPTER IV.

Paoli.

The King of Corsica was dead and buried in a foreign land, but other patriots, who fiercely loved their country, and as fiercely hated the Genoese, had risen to fill his place, and amongst these was Pasquale Paoli, probably the greatest patriot, the greatest friend of his country, and the best beloved of all Corsicans since the history of the country began. He had been carefully educated in Naples, where his father lived in exile. Pasquale was asked by the Corsicans, through his brother Clement, to become their General, and at the age of 29, in the year 1755, he was made Virtual Dictator of the island. His success was as remarkable as his measures were wise. Elections were regulated so that strong organisation was introduced into the loose democratic institutions which had hitherto prevented sufficient unity of action in troubled times. An army was raised from the straggling bands of volunteers, and brigandage was sternly suppressed.

Long struggles with the Genoese had made the people savage, revengeful and lawless. Agriculture and industries of all kinds were neglected. The Vendetta—the revenge for blood—was at its height, and one of the first laws made by Paoli was to punish the Vendettists with the pillory and death by the hangman, and for the time he cleared Corsica of its family feuds. The power of the Genoese was weakened day by day, agriculture had improved, and manufactures were established.

In 1765 Paoli opened the Corsican University at Corte. In it, theology, philosophy, mathematics, law and other sciences were taught. Paoli never wearied of labouring in many good causes, and he was looked up to as the father of his country. The Genoese saw that their reign must end, for the defence of the island had also been well and systematically looked to during these years. They concluded to sell the country—which in no way belonged to them—to France. The compact was signed at Versailles in May, 1768, and thus, as one writer observes, "a free people, with a most moral and civilised political constitution, was bartered away like a passive herd of cattle."

By this treaty it was agreed that the King of France should take and keep possession of the island till the Republic should be in a position to reimburse him the expense of sending an army of 30,000 men to subdue the island, and of maintaining garrisons there for several years, which it was foreseen they neither could, nor would repay. This equivocal mode of procedure at once saved the Genoese the reproaches of Italy for having sold Corsica to a foreign power, and furnished the French Minister with a pretext for retracting, in case the English should object to the new arrangement, for Louis XVI was averse to a war with England; but England at this time, uneasy at the disposition to revolt which manifested itself in the American colonies, had no desire to interfere on a feeling of pure disinterested generosity, the example of which might be turned against herself. When France became Republican, then it became an object to detach Corsica from her at any cost. But that was a widely different question.

The Duke of Choiseul made splendid overtures to Paoli to persuade the Corsicans to declare themselves a province of France, but these offers were rejected with disdain. He convoked the Council and laid before them the critical state of affairs. A youth of twenty deputed to the Council (Charles Buonaparte, the father of Napoleon), decided its resolution by a speech imbued with the noblest sentiments of antiquity. There was but one cry—"Liberty or Death." The conduct of the French Government excited the strongest reprobation. Some, indeed, gave a different turn to affairs; they said "Their ancestors had resisted the tyranny of the oligarchy of Genoa; they were now freed from it for ever. If Giafferis, Hyacinth, Paoli, Gaffori, Orticone, and the other lofty-minded men who had fallen in defence of their rights, could now see their country united to the finest monarchy in Europe, they would feel satisfied, and no longer regret the blood they had shed for her independence. By accepting the protection of Louis they would secure all the privileges of French subjects, and have the commerce of the ports of Europe thrown open to them." But these arguments had little effect; the people and their leaders were alike deaf to them. "We are invincible in our mountains;" they said, "there, let us remain and laugh at our enemies. They talk of the advantages we should obtain by submission; we have no ambition for them. We wish to remain poor, but free; our own masters, governed by our own laws and customs, and not the sport of a clerk from Versailles. They talk of the privileges to which we might be admitted—the privilege of becoming vassal to a despot. *As wills the King, so wills the law;* such is the maxim of the French monarchy. What security then is it likely to afford against the caprice and rapacity of a subaltern?" And the cry of "Liberty or Death" rang through the valleys of Corsica, and was echoed from her mountain tops. The mass of people who dwelt in the mountains had no notion of the power of France. They thought a few straggling regiments which they had seen, comprised the whole of the French armies. The public in France were also averse to a war with Corsica. "What had they to do with Corsica? Had it never existed till now? Why then, was it now thought of for the first time?" Besides, there seemed to be something cowardly in directing the power of a great nation against a handful of poor but spirited mountaineers. The expedition under Chauvelin with 12,000 men also failed; and his troops after the defeat at Borgo, were glad to retire into the fortresses. The Corsicans believed their deliverance accomplished. Clubs were formed in London that sent arms and money. Even Louis XVI was somewhat friendly, and shewed no haste to set this new crown on his head, until it was represented to him, how glad the French philosophers would be to see *Grand Monarque* foiled and compelled to retreat before a free people; there was no longer room for deliberation. The dread of opinion is the spring that had moved the politics of Europe for the last sixty years. Thirty thousand men under Marshall De Vaux set sail for Corsica in 1768. The Corsicans made a brave but ineffectual resistance. The passage of the Golo was manfully disputed step by step. Not having time to cut down the bridge, which was of stone, they made use of the bodies of their dead to form a rampart. Paoli, driven southwards, embarked in an English ship at Porto-Vecchio, landed at Leghorn, crossed the continent and hastened to London. He was everywhere received with tokens of admiration and respect, both by the people and their princes.

It was not expected that the Corsicans would resist the numbers sent against them. At one time Marshal De Vaux had imprudently dispersed his troops, thinking the country subdued, and had Paoli fallen on the French army thus disintegrated, he might have cut them to pieces, but he lacked the military tact and promptitude for executing so bold an enterprise. Five years afterwards (1774) an insurrection was raised in Nioli, a piéve among the peaks of the highest mountains. The Count de Narbonne made the French name odious by the cruelties he committed on this occasion, burning the dwellings, cutting down the olive and chesnut trees, and pulling up the vines. In 1790 the revolution produced a great alteration in the disposition of the people—they became reconciled to the French. Paoli then left England, where he had been living in exile, passed through Paris, where he was most flatteringly received, and returned to his own country after an absence of twenty years. The whole island flocked to see him—his arrival caused a general rejoicing. He was invested with the chief power in the island, and became at once exceedingly popular. However, a new era had arrived, and he did not perceive that many who had followed him into exile were now most refractory. His opinion of the revolution wavered after the well-known 10th of August, and the death of Louis XVI completed his dissatisfaction. He was denounced by the popular societies of Provençe, and the National Convention summoned him to Paris. This was an invitation to lay his head on the scaffold. He refused to go, and was declared guilty of high treason. He appealed to his countrymen, and prevailed on them to revolt against the Convention.

He determined to put Corsica under the protection of the English, and it was arranged that

Bust of Napoleon by Canova.

Admiral Hood, then in command of the English fleet near Toulon, should invade the island. Twelve thousand men, under the orders of Horatio Nelson, landed at San Fiorenzo; Paoli, with six thousand more, surrounded Bastia, which fell after a siege of four months.

In the month of June, 1794, Sir Gilbert Elliott was appointed Viceroy. He soon quarrelled with Paoli, who declared in a pique—"This is my kingdom. I carried on war against the King of France for two years; I expelled the Republicans. If you violate the privileges and rights of the kingdom, I can more easily expel you than I did them." He had expected to be chosen governor, and was extremely disappointed and chagrined to find others placed in authority over him. Sir Gilbert Elliott advised George III. to recall Paoli. After some hesitation he returned to London, where he died in 1807 at the age of eighty-two.

In less than two years another Corsican, the great Napoleon, set to work to oust the English, and the people, being exasperated by the recalling of their "Father" Paoli, gave him all assistance, and thus an island, to which we had no right, slipped back into the hands of the French nation, who have held it to the present time.

CHAPTER V.

Ajaccio.

It is said that the ancient town of Ajaccio derived its name from the hero Ajax; others from Ajazzo, the son of the Trojan prince, Corso, who wandered with Æneas to the Western Sea, carried off Sica, a niece of Dido, and thus gave the island the name of Corsica.

According to Ptolemy, the ancient town of Urcinium, which is said to be the Adjacium of the earliest part of the Middle Ages, lay on the Gulf of Ajaccio; and this town is always coupled with the oldest towns of the island, Aleria, Mariana, Nebium, and Sagona; it stood on the hill San Giovanni, to the north of the modern town, and where, formerly, were to be seen the ruins of the old cathedral, in which the bishops of Ajaccio long continued to be consecrated; now, nothing remains to show that a town once existed there. Many old Roman ruins were found in the vineyards, and in

Avenue leading from the Quay of Ajaccio.

them large vessels of terra cotta of an oval shape, probably sepulchral urns, as skeletons were often found in them.

The new town was founded by the Bank of St. George, of Genoa, in the year 1492. It was the seat of a lieutenant, or vicegerent of the Governor of Bastia, and was not raised to the dignity of Capital of the island till 1811, at the request of Madame Letitia and Cardinal Fesch, in honour of its being the birthplace of the Buonapartes.

A broad stone quay forms a frontage to modern Ajaccio; from thence an avenue of palms and plane trees leads up to the town; rows of tall, plain, massive buildings curve round the great bay; there is no beauty of architecture about them, yet their colour, their light façades, and gray Venetian blinds, blending with the foliage of orange trees, give the main street, Cours Napoléon, a rich and picturesque appearance.

The names of the streets and squares are essentially Napoleonic—Cours Napoléon, Rue Napoléon, Rue Fesch, Rue Cardinal, Place Letitia, and Rue du Roi de Rome. The memory of Napoleon is indeed the soul of the town, and one lounges from street to street buried in thoughts of that wonderful man and his childhood. Parallel with the Cours

Napoléon runs the Rue Fesch. The former leads to the broad Place du Diamant, which lies on the sea coast, and commands a fine view of the gulf and its southern shore.

In the Grande Place, facing the sea, there is a fine equestrian statue of Napoleon, surrounded by those of the four kings, his brothers: Joseph, Jerome, Lucien, and Louis. These statues were erected by national subscription. In the market-place, which leads to the harbour, there is a large cube of marble surmounted by a statue of Napoleon, on an extravagantly high pedestal, on which one reads the following inscription:—" To the Emperor Napoleon, his native town (dedicates this statue) May 5, 1850. In the second year of the Presidency of Louis Napoleon." The extraordinary part of the story connected with this statue is, that it was not Napoleon at all, but a statue of Ganymede, sent by the family of Buonaparte to Signor Ramolino, but as the people saw it landed from the ship, they took the eagle of Ganymede for the imperial eagle, and Ganymede for Napoleon, so they collected in the market-place, and demanded that the statue should be set there, so that they might have the great Napoleon in marble in their midst. In converting the Trojan youth, Ganymede, into their

Statue of Napoleon.

countryman, Napoleon, the honest Corsicans seem surely to have verified the chronicler's fable that the Ajaccines are derived from a Trojan prince.

The statue is only a mediocre work of Laboureur, but its position in the face of the gulf enhances its local effect. It is a consular statue, wearing the Roman toga, with a laurel wreath on its head. In its right hand is a rudder, which rests on the globe of the world. The idea is a happy one, for in sight of the gulf the rudder is a perfectly natural symbol, and doubly appropriate in the hands of the islanders. For memory roves from the marketplace to the sea, and beholds the ship which brought Napoleon from Egypt to France at anchor in the gulf. He sat on board there by night, and hastily skimmed all the newspapers they could find for him in Ajaccio; and here it was that he formed the mighty resolution of seizing that rudder by which he was to govern not France alone, but an empire and half the world, until it broke in his hands, and the man of Corsica was wrecked on the rocks of the island of St. Helena.

One side of the market-place, which looks on the bay, is bounded by a solid granite quay, on the other side is a row of tall, well-built houses. The view of the blue bay, with its semicircle of grand mountains in the distance, is indescribably beautiful from this point. This magnificent bay is protected on its western side by a granite mole, designed by Napoleon.

The late Emperor (Napoleon III), and especially his cousin Louis Napoleon, had strong Corsican sympathies. The latter had an estate near Calvi, which he frequently visited for shooting. Under their auspices, the town began to show that it really is the birthplace of an imperial dynasty. A very chaste and beautiful chapel has been built as the mausoleum of several members of the imperial family. A museum and picture gallery has also been erected. In it, carefully arranged, is a large gallery of paintings left to Ajaccio by Cardinal Fesch, which had long been stowed away in lumber rooms. Some of the pictures are good, but the greater number are only second-rate.

In the town hall there is a salon, called the Buonaparte Museum, here are many mementoes of Napoleon, family portraits, pictures and interesting busts, among the latter that of Napoleon, by Canova, the beautiful bust of Madame Letitia, Cardinal Fesch, and a small one of the infant king of Rome. There is also a bronze cast of the head of Napoleon, taken after death. The town hall boasts of a library

of over 27,000 volumes, the foundation of which was laid by Lucien Buonaparte. The Préfecture also possesses a valuable library, the shelves of which are especially rich in archives and documents important to Corsican history.

Ajaccio is very poor in public institutions and buildings. Its most important edifice is the house of the Buonapartes.

CHAPTER VI.

The House of the Buonapartes.

The great and mysterious charm about this little southern town is its having been the birthplace of Napoleon. It was here that he spent his childhood and early youth, until, at the age of fifteen, he entered the military school of Brienne.

Out of the Rue Napoleon, a narrow street (Rue Charles) leads to a small square, and opposite this stands an old fashioned three storied house, with a gallery on its flat roof. Like most houses in Corsica it is stuccoed, and totally devoid of ornament; its many windows are protected with gray Venetian-blind shutters, opening on either side. On the corner of this house you read the inscription: *Place Letitia.*

No one knows when the house was built, probably when Genoa governed the island, and Louis XIV filled the world with the glory of himself and France. When the architect planned this house he little thought that capricious fortune would shower

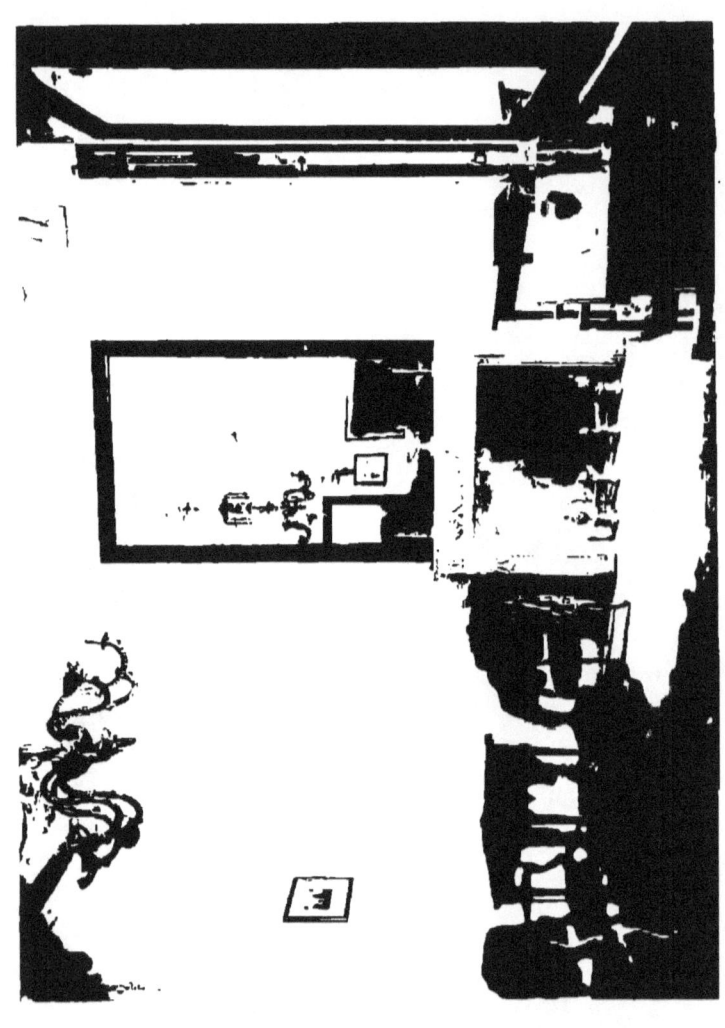

The Office of his father (Charles Buonaparte) in House of the Buonapartes.

Sedan Chair belonging to Madame Letitia in House of the Buonapartes

Room where Napoleon was born in House of the Buonapartes.

The House of the Buonapartes.

imperial and royal crowns upon its roof, and that it would be the cradle of a race of princes who should swallow up whole countries. In this house, on February 8th, 1769, Napoleon was born. His mother had gone to church (being the Festival of Assumption), but finding herself taken ill, was hastily brought home in her sedan chair, which she reached just in time, and she was delivered of the future conqueror upon a temporary couch prepared for her accommodation, covered with an ancient piece of tapestry, representing the story of the heroes of the *Iliad*, and the little bed in which the infant was placed still remains in the same corner of the room.

The house is now the property of the ex-Empress Eugénie. No one lives in it, but it is kept in good order, as a show-place and historic museum. After ascending the first flight of stairs you enter the parlour, with its tiled floor; here is Madame Letitia's spinet standing open, its yellow time-worn keys tempting one to play thereon. The ancient wires emit sounds "like sweet bells, jangled and out of tune." Now you enter what was once the study or office of the notary—the father of the family. Here there is a good carved mantelpiece and some fine specimens of inlaid marquetry furniture, among them the desk at which he was wont to sit and write. A pretty little bust of the late Prince Imperial stands in the birth-room of Napoleon, placed there by the ex-Empress Eugénie. This is a little room lined with blue tapestry, with two windows, one of which looks on a balcony towards the court, the other towards the street. One sees in it a cupboard in the wall, behind a tapestried door, and a fireplace bordered with yellow marble, and decorated by a few mythological bas-reliefs. The ball-room, with its polished marquetry floor, is the finest room in the house. There are antique chairs, and mirrors with sconces for candles adorn the walls. The windows on one side open on to a garden terrace, where there is trellis work beautified by a wealth of creepers and flowers; but of view there is none, the windows of other houses overlook it. Now let us enter Napoleon's little bedroom and his working room. The two cupboards are still to be seen in which his school books were kept. A trap door is also pointed out, through which he is said to have escaped when pursued by Paoli's troops. Excited fancy seeks them all in these rooms, and sees them assembled round their mother — ordinary children, like other men's children, schoolboys toiling at their Plutarch or Cæsar, tutored by their

Ball Room in House of the Buonapartes.

grave father and their great-uncle, Lucien ; and the three sisters growing up careless and rather wild, like their neighbours in the half barbarous town There is Joseph the eldest, then *Napoleon*, Lucien, Louis, Jerome, also Caroline, Eliza, and Pauline, the children of a notary of moderate income, who is incessantly and vainly carrying on lawsuits with the Jesuits of Ajaccio, to gain a contested estate which is necessary to his numerous family. For the future of his children fills him with anxiety. What will they be in the world, and how shall they secure a comfortable subsistence ?

CHAPTER VII.

NAPOLEON.

Now let us turn to the advent of her greatest son, whose stupendous intellect was soon to humble in the dust the crowned kings and emperors of Europe, whose restless energy strove to conquer a continent had not another mighty intellect arisen whose like energy checked a career which met its utter downfall on the field of Waterloo.

Napoleon Buonaparte was the fourth son of Charles Buonaparte, advocate, and of Letitia Ramolino, his wife, a Corsican lady of great beauty and of good family. She was a typical Corsican, a peasant to the last day of her long life—lowly, frugal, and somewhat unscrupulous. She was of heroic mould, and probably to his mother Napoleon owed his extraordinary physical endurance. The peasant mother was most prolific. Her eldest child, born in 1765, was a son, who died in infancy; in 1767 a daughter, who also died; in 1768 a son, known as Joseph; in 1769 *Napoleon*. Nine other children were born, six of whom survived to share

Bust of Madame Letitia (Napoleon's Mother.)

their brother's greatness. Their mother lived to the ripe age of eighty-six, in full enjoyment of her faculties, known to the world as *Madame Mère.*

Gregorovius, speaking of the family of the notary of Ajaccio, says, "And behold these same children, one after the other take to themselves the mightiest crowns of the earth. Napoleon is European Emperor; Joseph, King of Spain; Louis, King of Holland; Jerome, King of Westphalia; Pauline, a princess of Italy; Eliza, a princess of Italy; Caroline, Queen of Naples. So many crowned potentates were born and educated in this little house by a lady unknown to fame, the daughter of a citizen of a small and seldom mentioned country town, Letitia Ramolino, who, at the age of fifteen, married a man equally unknown. Even history is a part of nature. There is in it a chain of cause and effect, and what we call genius in a man is always the result of definite conditions. An almost unbroken contest of more than a thousand years between Corsica and her tyrants had preceded before the great conqueror Napoleon was born, in whose nature this rock-bound island and this energetic and battle-proof island people, pressed close in a narrow space of ground, produced for themselves an organ whose law was boundlessness. This is the upward series—*the Corsican bandit, the Corsican soldier, Renuccio della Rocca, Sampiero, Gaffori, Pasquali Paoli, Napoleon.*"

The name of Buonaparte was often spelt indiscriminately, with the *u* or without it, by the different branches of the family. Sometimes it has happened that of two brothers one has spelt it one way and the other the other. The omission of this letter was common in very early times.

The name was spelt *Buonaparte* during his first Italian campaign, but when he returned to Paris, covered with glory, he dropped the Italian orthography, and, to render it more nearly French, wrote it henceforth Bonaparte.

The Christian name of Napoleon has also been made a subject of dispute. It was frequent in the Orsini and Lomellini families, from whom it was taken by that of Buonaparte. It was always given to the second son. The correct way of writing it is *Napoleone*. Some pretend that it is derived from the Greek, and signifies *Lion of the Desert*; others, that it is derived from the Latin. This name is not to be found in the Roman calendar. From researches made in the Martyrologies at Rome at the period of the establishment of the Concordat, it appears that St. Napoleon was a Greek martyr.

Clarke, afterwards Duke of Feltré (who was proud of his Irish extraction), when sent ambassador to Florence, busied himself with inquiries into Buonaparte's pedigree, to which the latter put a stop by saying, *I am the first of my family*; and to the Emperor of Austria, who, at the time of his marriage with his daughter, set the heralds to work to trace his genealogy to the old Italian nobility, he answered much in the same spirit, that "*he would rather be the son of a peasant than descended from any of the petty tyrants of Italy.*"

The origin of the Buonaparte family cannot be precisely ascertained. A pedigree has been constructed, beginning with Emmanuel II, the eighth Greek Emperor of the house of the Commeni. whose two sons are said to have emigrated under the name of Buonaparte after the fall of Constantinople, first to Corfu, then to Naples, Rome and Florence. From them, fiction will have it, that the Corsican Buonapartes are descended. The Buonapartes played no part in Corsican history. Influential in their own town, they confined themselves to a share in civic administration of the town. It was not till Carlo Buonaparte, Napoleon's father, that the name acquires consideration throughout Corsica, and becomes to a certain extent historic.

CHAPTER VIII.

Napoleon's Childhood.

LITTLE is known of Napoleon's early childhood except what he himself relates. He was not christened till July, 1771, nearly two years after his birth, and then he was baptised together with his sister, Maria Anna, who died soon after. They say he struggled violently when the priest besprinkled him with holy water. Perhaps he wanted to baptise himself, as he afterwards crowned himself, taking the crown out of the hands of the Pope, who was going to put it on his head.

As a boy, he displayed a violent and passionate temper, and was constantly quarrelling with his elder brother Joseph. Napoleon relates the following of his childhood. He says he was nothing more than an obstinate and inquisitive child.

"In my infancy I was extremely headstrong; nothing overawed me, nothing disconcerted me. I was quarrelsome, mischievous. I was afraid of nobody; I beat one, I scratched another; I made myself formidable to the whole family. My brother Joseph was the one with whom I was oftenest embroiled, he was beaten, bitten, abused. I went to complain before he had time to recover from his confusion. I had need to be on the alert; our mother would have repressed my warlike humour, she would not have put up with my caprices. Her tenderness was joined with severity; she punished, rewarded all alike; the good, the bad, nothing escaped her. My father, a man of sense, but too fond of pleasure to pay much attention to our infancy, sometimes attempted to excuse our faults: 'Let them alone,' she replied, 'It is not your business, it is I who must look after them.' She did, indeed, watch over us with a solicitude unexampled. Every low sentiment, every ungenerous affection was discarded, discouraged; she suffered nothing but what was grand and elevating to take root in our youthful understandings. She abhorred falsehoods, was provoked by disobedience; she passed over none of our faults. I recollect a mischance which befel me in this way, and the punishment which was inflicted on me. We had some fig-trees in a vineyard; we used to climb them; we might meet with a fall, and accidents; she forbade us to go near them without her knowledge. This prohibition gave me a good deal of uneasiness; but it had been pronounced, and I attended to it. One day, however, I was idle, and at a loss for something to do, I took it into my head to long for some of those figs. They were ripe; no one saw me, or could know anything of the matter; I made my escape, ran to the tree, and gathered the whole. My appetite being satisfied, I was providing for the future by filling my pockets when an unlucky vineyard keeper came in sight. I was half dead with fear, and remained fixed on the branch of the tree where he had surprised me. He wished to seize and conduct me to my mother. Despair rendered me eloquent. I represented my distress, undertook to keep away from the figs in future, was prodigal of assurances, and he seemed satisfied. I congratulated myself on having come off so well, and fancied that the adventure would not transpire, but the traitor told all. The next day, Signora Letitia wanted to go and gather some figs. I had not left any, there were none to be found, the keeper came, great reproaches followed, and an exposure; the culprit had to expiate his fault."

The family seems even at an early time to have regarded Napoleon as the head of the children. Archdeacon Lucien on his deathbed, said to Joseph,

Napoleon's Childhood.

" Thou art the eldest of the family, but yonder is the head; thou must not forget this."

When he was six years old he was placed in a school with some little girls; they all made much of him; but he always had his stockings down about his heels, and in walking out he never let go the hand of a charming girl, who was the occasion of many quarrels with other boys, who, jealous of his Giacominetta, connected the two circumstances together, and put them into song. He never appeared in the street but they followed him, repeating the rhymes: "Napoleone di mezza calzetta, fa l'amore a Giacominetta."*

He could not bear to be made sport of. He seized sticks, stones, everything that came in his way, and rushed furiously among the throng. Fortunately someone was always by to put an end to the affair, and bring him safe out of it; for numbers did not intimidate him, he never stopped to count adversaries.

As a boy, Napoleon displayed an irresistible passion for everything military, and this born soldier liked nothing better than running along beside the military in Ajaccio. He teased his father with entreaties to buy him a cannon; and long subse-

* Napoleon with his stockings half off, makes love to Giacominetta.

quently, they showed in the Buonaparte house the little metal cannon with which he used to play.

Napoleon also related the following to his fellow countryman Antommarchi: "I came into the world in the arms of old Mammuccia Caterina. She was obstinate, captious, continually at war with all around her. She was perpetually quarrelling with my grandmother, of whom, notwithstanding, she was very fond, and who had the same regard for her. Yet she was kind, affectionate; she walked out with us, took care of us, made us laugh; she showed an anxiety for us, the recollection of which is not yet effaced. I still remember the tears she shed when I quitted Corsica. That is now forty years ago. You were not then born; I was young and did not foresee the glory that awaited me, still less that we should find ourselves here together;* but destiny is unchangeable, one must obey one's star. Mine was to run through the extremes of life: and I set out to fulfil the task assigned me."

* At St. Helena.

CHAPTER IX.

Napoleon's Schooldays.

At the school at Brienne it has been said that his poverty exposed him to mortification, to which he was forced to submit in silence, but with inward indignation, in the midst of boys more favoured by fortune than himself. Reports were also spread, injurious to the character of his mother and the profession of his father, which on more than one occasion drove him beyond the bounds of patience and discretion. He was alternately accused of being a son of a Corsican attorney, and next of Monsieur Marbœuf, the French Governor, sent over to Corsica, though the latter only arrived in the island in June, 1769, three months after the birth of Napoleon. The spirit which Napoleon had shown in vindication of the honour of his parents procured him many friends in the school. One day one of the teachers, not attending to the character of the child, had condemned him to wear a coarse woollen dress, and to dine on his knees at the door of the refectory. This, the young Corsican's pride could not brook; it brought on a sudden vomiting and a violent fit of hysterics. The superior, who was passing by chance, snatched him from his intended punishment; and Father Patrault, the mathematical professor, complained bitterly that they should thus degrade his first mathematician. He seldom joined in the sports of the other boys, but shut himself up with a volume of Plutarch, or some work on history; probably the want of exercise and recreation stunted his growth, for his body was not proportioned to his remarkably fine manly head, cast in the mould of the antique. The games in which he indulged at this early period, it was remarked, were images of war; he saw himself surrounded with camps, fortifications, armies, and already played the conqueror and hero in battle. In the winter of 1783, the pupils constructed a regular fort with snow. Buonaparte took a great share in this important concern; the fort was alternately attacked, taken, retaken; and he showed, both in the attack and defence, equal courage, hardihood and address.

Stubborn and intractable with his equals, he was docile to his superiors, and never rebelled against established authority. A love of order, or sense of the value of power, whether in himself or others, seems to have been always a first principle in his mind. Diligent, studious and grave, he became a favourite with his teachers. His chief studies were history and mathematics: the one taught him a knowledge of mankind, as the other put instruments into his hands for mastering them. Seeking neither for relaxation or amusement, he applied himself closely to those several branches of study which rested on positive grounds and led to practical results. Madame De Brienne used to invite several of the schoolboys, and among them Napoleon, to visit her at her chateau. It is to her that he is supposed to have returned the characteristic answer addressed to some lady of quality who was complaining of the burning of the Palatinate by the great Turenne, "And why not, Madame, if it was necessary to his designs?" In the campaign of 1814, the victory was bloodily contested with Blucher in the chateau de Brienne, foot to foot, and chamber to chamber, on the very spot where he was brought up, which must have been a very mortifying reflection to him. In the year 1783 he was sent to the military school at Paris, being one of the best three scholars, chosen annually from each of the twelve provincial schools of France. His masters entertained a high opinion of his ability, so much so that Leguille, professor of history at Paris, predicted his subsequent career. In fact, to the name of Buonaparte, was appended the following note:—"*A Corsican by birth and character—he will do something great if circumstances favour him.*" In 1785, he was examined by the celebrated mathematician, La Place, and obtained the brevet of a second lieutenant of artillery in the regiment of La Fère; he was then sixteen years of age.

When stationed at Valenu, he fell in love with the daughter of Madame du Colombier, a girl of his own age, but it came to nothing more than their walking out together, planning stolen interviews, and eating most harmless cherries.

Now and then he visited Ajaccio, and he was fond of living and working at Milelli, a small country house, near the town, belonging to his mother. In its grounds there is an old oak tree, and a spot sheltered by huge rocks, now called Napoleon's Grotto, where he used to sit and dream or meditate. It was here he wrote his celebrated manifesto, which was an insight into the nature of the growth and development of the future emperor. Then came the French Revolution, the assault of the Bastille, and the downfall of the existing state of things.

Young Napoleon threw himself into the in-

tellectual movement with the whole passion of his nature. We find him in Ajaccio a young ardent revolutionist, making speeches in the clubs, writing addresses, helping to organise the national guard—in a word, playing the great politician.

Ajaccio was at that time the centre of the Corsican revolutionists: the Buonaparte house soon became their place of meeting, and the brothers Joseph and Napoleon decided leaders of the democracy. The little town became wild with excitement and confusion. Napoleon and Joseph assembled the democratic party in the church of San Francisco, and drew up a letter of congratulation to the constituent assembly, in which, at the same time, the bitterest complaints were expressed against the existing administration of Corsica, and the demand was made that Corsica might be declared an integral part of France.

Napoleon perceived his time had come; renouncing his Corsican patriotism, he became a decided Frenchman, and from this time onward he looked to France for his career.

The narrow horizon of his native island was no longer wide enough for him, but from its bracing mountain air, and from the quick blood of his race, he drew a magnetic force which imparted to his decisions a rapidity and energy that carried all before them, while at the same time a power of calm calculation, of industry, and of self-control enabled him to employ his genius to the best advantage. The force of his personality was so overwhelming that, in considering his career, the regret must ever be present that the only principle that remained steadfast with him, and is the key to his conduct throughout, should have been the care for his own advancement, glory and power.

FINIS.

www.ingramcontent.com/pod-product-compliance
Lightning Source LLC
Chambersburg PA
CBHW030401170426
43202CB00010B/1455